Country Seasons Coloring Book

Thank you for choosing Ava Browne Coloring Books.
We strive to publish unique coloring books for all ages.

Visit us at www.Avabrowne.com and sign up to our free newsletter. All new subscribers receive a FREE 10 Page PDF Coloring Book!

**Join our active and growing Facebook Community at www.facebook.com/groups/avabrownecoloring
All group members receive a FREE 20 Page PDF Coloring Book!**

If you found this coloring book enjoyable, please leave us a review.

Reviews help drive sales which allows us to make more coloring books.

www.avabrowne.com

This book also includes a free digital copy that you can print out at home. For instructions and your access code, please go to the last page.

Find us on social media:
facebook.com/groups/avabrownecoloring
https://www.instagram.com/ava_browne_coloring/

If you have any questions please contact us at:
Ava@avabrowne.com

Thank you and happy coloring!

SCAN ME FOR FREE PAGES!

FACEBOOK

EMAIL SIGN UP

COLOR TEST PAGE

COLOR TEST PAGE

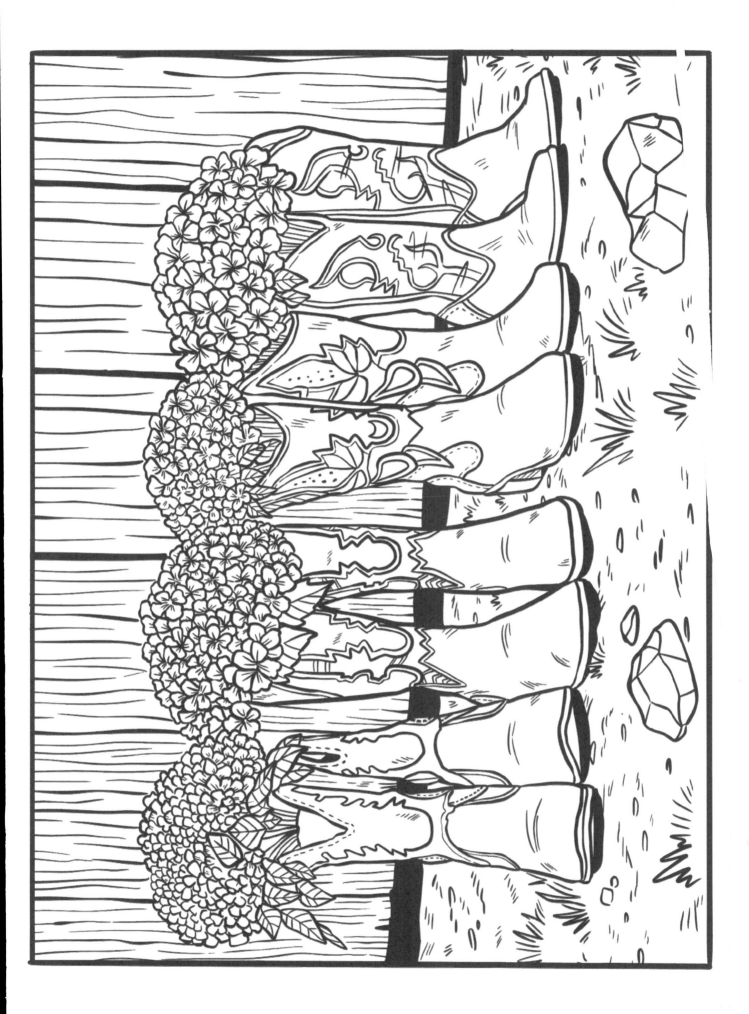

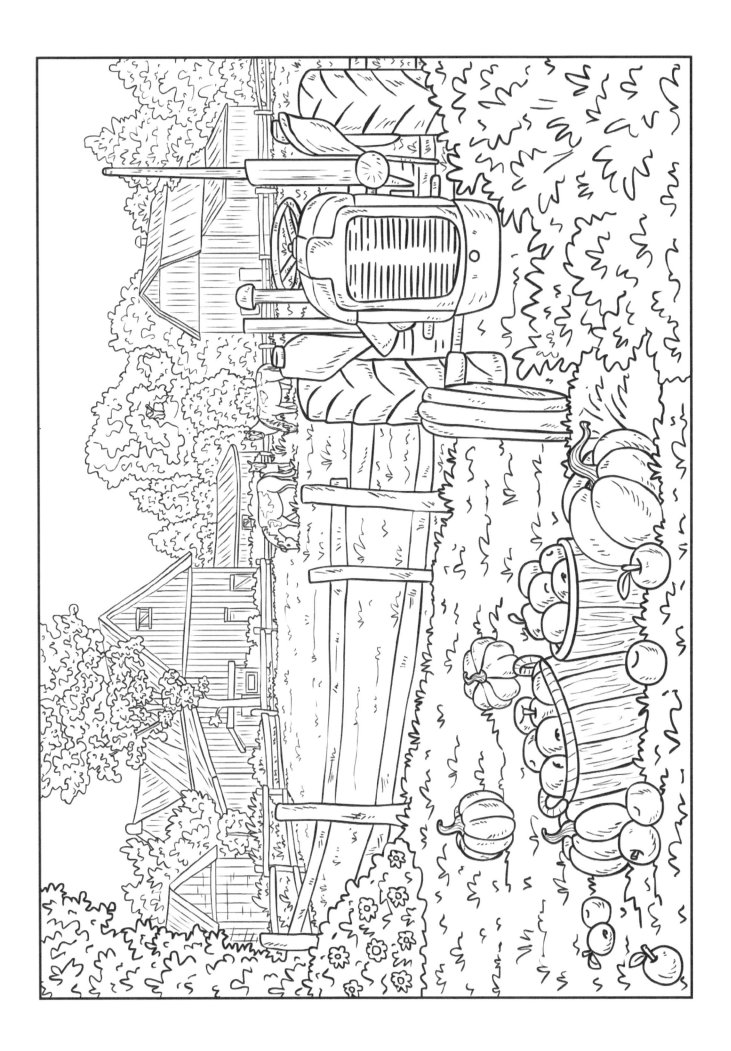

Please visit
https://avabrowne.com/country-seasons-download/
to download your free digital copy.

Please consider subscribing to our newsletter, and
enter the password

kaaaayjs

to access the file.(All Lowercase)

Made in United States
Troutdale, OR
04/14/2024

19174156R00117